Bygone Scone
Guthrie Hutton

A cottage at Scone photographed in 1910.

© 2006 Guthrie Hutton
First Published in the United Kingdom, 2006
Stenlake Publishing Limited
54–58 Mill Square, Catrine, KA5 6RD
www.stenlake.co.uk

ISBN 9781840333862

ACKNOWLEDGEMENTS

For a place of such significance it is surprising that so little has been published on Scone, and writing a modest little book like this can only scratch the surface of what remains to be discovered. My task was considerably eased by the staff at the A. K. Bell Library, Perth, who were not just a great help, but cheery and friendly also. Amongst other material, the library holds an unpublished typescript of research done in 1964 by the women of Scone SWRI for which they should be commended and congratulated. More work has been done locally by the Scone Historical Society which held a splendid exhibition to mark the 200th anniversary of the village in 2005. It proved to be valuable both as a source of information and photographs. The pictures on pages 18, 30 and 41 came from the exhibition and I must thank Mike Moir of the Society for his help with these. I am grateful too to Denholm T. Reid, Alan Brotchie and Stewart Donaldson for their help in providing illustrations.

The road linking Old and New Scone villages is seen here in the mid-1920s at its junction with the Perth to Blairgowrie road at Old Scone. The gate facing the road end is a driveway into Scone Palace.

FURTHER READING

Breeze, David and Munro, Graeme, *The Stone of Destiny*, 1997.
Dow, John, *New Scone*: *The By-gone Life*, 1902 (reprinted).
Haynes, Nick, *Perth & Kinross: An Illustrated ArchitecturalGuide*, 2000.
Scone Palace, various guidebooks.
Watson, Norman, *Perth in Old Picture Postcards*, 1993.

Also by Guthrie Hutton for Stenlake Publishing:
Old Perth, 1995.
Bygone Perth, 2005.
Old Kinross-shire, 2003 (with David Millar).

INTRODUCTION

Scone occupies a special place in Scottish history. It is regarded as the former Pictish capital and the place where rulers of that ancient kingdom were crowned. After the Picts were ousted in AD 843 by the king of Scots, Kenneth macAlpine, Scone became the place where Scotland's monarchs were crowned. For these ceremonies they sat on a large stone, sometimes known as the Stone of Destiny. The stone's turbulent past has elevated it to iconic status for some Scots, although its origins and history have long been the subject of debate.

There are people who think it came from Iona, but others have claimed a more distant and magical source for it, while geologists have declared it to be a type of old red sandstone found in the locality. King Edward I of England forcibly removed the stone in 1296, but the identity of what he took has been hotly debated. Some people believe that the real stone was spirited away and hidden before Edward arrived and that he carted off a fake to London. For centuries, therefore, the stone that sat beneath the Coronation Chair in Westminster Abbey may not have been the real thing. This begs the question, if it wasn't genuine why was the real one not produced for the coronation of King Robert the Bruce in 1306? The four young Scots who got into the Abbey on Christmas Eve 1950 and removed the stone from beneath the chair must have thought it was genuine, but this daring adventure spawned another rash of theories. Was the stone that was eventually returned to the Abbey the real thing or another fake? (The author saw one of the many supposed copies still lying in a Glasgow stonemason's yard in the 1960s and, while that and others could have been passed off as the actual stone, the concrete block displayed on a bogie at Fallin Colliery only served to illustrate the fun people had putting about hoaxes at that time.)

The stone was ceremonially returned to Scotland in 1996, 700 years after it had been taken south by Edward I, and is now kept in Edinburgh Castle. Experts have declared it to be the real stone, but the question of whether or not it is the one sat on at Scone by Scottish kings will fuel many a pub debate and keep conspiracy theorists happy for years to come. What is not

The students who took the Stone of Destiny from Westminster Abbey on Christmas Eve 1950 left it the following April at Arbroath Abbey, wrapped in a Saltire.

Scone Palace, erected on the site of the old Bishop's Palace, as it appeared in 1775.

The medieval mercat cross and graveyard are the only surviving elements of the old village. The cross has been resited on a small earth knoll close to the graveyard, which is now somewhat overgrown and tumble-down.

in dispute is that it must be one of the best-known bits of stone in the world and Scone must be equally well known because it gets a mention every time the stone is talked about.

This fame by association with the stone has, however, tended to overshadow the rest of Scone's history, and the progressive disappearance of much of the evidence hasn't helped either. The place where those coronations were held was the Abbey, one of the foremost religious houses in Scotland. Alongside was the Bishop's Palace, where visiting monarchs would stay. Cheek by jowl with these great buildings was the township inhabited by ordinary folk, whose lives were no doubt geared to serving the religious community. The church was therefore a centre of power, waited on by lesser mortals and attended by kings, but all that changed in one cataclysmic event: the Reformation. In 1559 John Knox preached a sermon in St John's Kirk in Perth in which he denounced idolatry. Inflamed by his words, the congregation went on the rampage, wrecking and pillaging the city's monasteries and church. Knox managed to stop them from going on to Scone, but when people in Dundee heard of the mayhem in Perth they decided to get a slice of the action and descended on Scone. In the ensuing confusion a man trying to steal beer was killed by a monk. It was the trigger for a riot during which the mob stripped the Abbey and

The sixteenth-century gateway, adorned with plaques bearing the arms of 1st Viscount Stormont and King James VI, is still in place. It gave access from the old village to the palace.

Palace of their riches and burned them to the ground. Scone's power, as well as its great buildings, had been destroyed.

The classic post-Reformation story then unfolded as church lands were distributed by the Crown among rich and powerful families. Scone was handed to the Ruthvens, who were dab hands at the kind of belligerent behaviour that in those days won vast wealth and property. They built a new palace on the site of the old Bishop's Palace about 1580, but blew their good fortune twenty years later in an event known as the Gowrie Conspiracy, which may or may not have threatened the life of King James VI. This incident is too complicated and intrigue-ridden to go into here, but the upshot of it was that the King confiscated Scone from the Ruthvens and bestowed it on Sir David Murray of Gospetrie, who had come to his rescue in the tumult after the conspiracy. The Murrays were not as careless as the Ruthvens. Sir David was made Lord Scone in 1605 and Viscount Stormont in 1621. His descendant, also David, 7th Viscount Stormont, became the 2nd Earl of Mansfield in 1793, a title he inherited from his uncle. The Earldom is the family's senior title, and Scone Palace is still in their possession.

So Edward I took the stone and the Dundee mob destroyed the Abbey and Palace, but perhaps the most remarkable disappearance of all has been the village itself. At the instigation of the 3rd Earl of Mansfield it was uprooted from its original site in the early nineteenth century and, as if by some Brigadoon-like magic, reappeared two miles away on the high ground to the east. It is one of the most dramatic and complete new town developments in Scotland's history, yet few people know about it. People moved, businesses moved, houses moved and churches moved stone by numbered stone. Many more stones were moved out of Scone in the early nineteenth century than in the late thirteenth, but it is the earlier event that has made the history books – a triumph, perhaps, of the Scots' taste for ancient blood-and-thunder history over the everyday struggle of ordinary people.

The village was initially known as New Scone, but is now usually just called Scone. It celebrated its 200th anniversary in 2005.

No sooner had Sir David Murray of Gospetrie taken possession of Scone, after the Gowrie Conspiracy of 1600, than he set about expanding the palace by adding new ranges to it. Thus extended, the building passed through the generations until it was inherited in 1796 by David William Murray, 3rd Earl of Mansfield. He began the process of remodelling the palace under the direction of the architect William Atkinson. The extensive work was carried out between 1803 and 1812 and, when completed, the structure looked more like one from the nineteenth century than a reflection of the earlier periods. Despite this, the early seventeenth-century long gallery, with its splendid oak and bog oak floor, is still perhaps the building's finest feature. While the palace was being improved, the grounds were being landscaped, and it was this process that led to the village being moved to its new site.

Scone woods, a large area of both planted and naturally regenerating trees, at one time stretched from the palace grounds up to New Scone at Sandy Road and Abbey Road. Such woodlands were common to large country estates and although many of these were stripped to meet the demands of the First World War, Scone's well-managed woods survived, albeit somewhat reduced. Forestry, however, owes a lot to Scone, or more precisely to a son of Scone, David Douglas, who was born on the estate in 1798. At the age of eleven he was apprenticed to the head gardener before moving to work at Glasgow's Botanical Gardens. There his talents attracted attention and he was chosen to go on a plant-hunting expedition to North America on behalf of the Horticultural Society of London (later the Royal Horticultural Society). He returned from that and subsequent expeditions with numerous plant species, particularly the conifers including Lodgepole Pine, Sitka Spruce and the one named after him, the Douglas Fir.

The grounds of the palace were made available to the army during the First World War for use as a training camp known as Scone Park Camp. The Gordon Highlanders were the first regiment to use it, in 1915. The soldiers shown on these two pages were at the camp the following year and are thought to belong to the 3rd Line Yeomanry Group. This was made up of a number of Territorial Army regiments which may explain why the men are wearing a variety of different uniforms. The pictures were used as postcards by a man from West Lothian ('Bob'), although it is not known if he is one of the group on this page. He was having a 'brisk time', had 'secured a very suitable job' and describes the July weather as salubrious.

A month later, at the end of August, Bob sent this card reporting that he was as 'happy as a bee', perhaps because the food was to his liking – he described this ragtag of ill-clothed soldiery as the 'boys responsible for our good cooking'. The 3rd Line Yeomanry Group was still at the camp in early September when a large sports meeting was held there. Other military units, like the Black Watch from Perth, took part alongside the Yeomen in a variety of events. The weather for the event was fine although, according to Bob it had 'broken down' in late August and the men would 'soon be up to the knees in mud'. The awful reality of pictures like these is that these men may indeed have shortly afterwards been up to their knees in the mud of the trenches, facing the kind of hell no bee or any other creature could be happy in!

When the main bulk of the community was decanted up the hill, a remnant continued in existence, strung out along the Perth to Blairgowrie Road. Although known as Old Scone, it is also in effect a new village of nineteenth-century estate workers' houses surrounded by trees. The main highway was created as a turnpike road, one of many toll roads made by private trusts in the late eighteenth and early nineteenth centuries in an attempt to improve transport links throughout the country. The road it replaced, which ran through the original village, is now the main drive to Scone Palace.

The cottages in these pictures from the 1920s are still there and, although modernised, are little altered. The trees, however, do seem bigger and the volume of traffic on the improved surface would make standing in the road a touch risky. The road leading off in the left foreground of the upper picture and on the right of the lower one goes past Perth racecourse to Waulkmill and Stormontfield.

Balboughty is a group of estate farm buildings half a mile beyond Old Scone on the Blairgowrie Road. They were built in the mid-nineteenth century and credited to the architect John MacDonald, although the Earl of Mansfield is also said to have had a hand in their design. The main elements are Balboughty House, seen here, and the adjacent steading. There is a square tower on the steading and each side has a different clock face: the one looking towards the road has, instead of numerals, the letters of the Mansfield motto: Spero Meliora; that facing north bears the Stormont motto: Uni Æquus Virtuti; on the southern dial is the national motto: Nemo Me Impune Lacessit; while the one facing west has simple roman numerals. A classical education would clearly have been useful for anyone working on Balboughty farm. Next to the 'big house' is the farmhouse, while across the road is the smithy, which has oddly oversized stone finials surmounting each gable. The most northerly of the buildings, Balboughty Cottages (below), on the same side of the road as the steading, appear to have changed little since these pictures were taken about 1905.

A couple of miles north of Old Scone is Waulkmill, sited at the confluence of the River Tay and St Martin's Burn. This was the location of a ferry across the river and, as the name suggests, the site of a mill. To the north is Stormontfield, which was formerly engaged in the bleaching and dyeing of cloth: the 'field' in the name refers to a bleachfield. The bleach works, which obtained its water by way of a canal led from the Tay, was initially operated by the Earl of Mansfield, but was purchased from him in 1925 by the firm of Lumsden & Mackenzie. The village had no shop or post office, but from 1897 it did have a church, which was built as a chapel of ease attached to Scone Parish Church. It also had a school which these serious-looking children attended in 1909.

Some folk say that Quarrymill is in Perth, others claim it for Scone, while in between are the inevitable 'don't knows'. The name is derived from the industries – quarrying and milling – that formerly used the natural resources of what has now reverted to being just the lovely wooded glen of the Annaty Burn. The burn flows past the southern edge of Scone and down past Scone Wood. Its course steepens as it gets closer to the Tay and this splendid combination of fast-flowing water and falling ground encouraged the development of mills: the remains of dams, ponds and lades can still be seen beside the burn. By the early years of the twentieth century Quarrymill was regarded as a pleasant place to walk, although the presence of a hermit seeking solitude suggests it had few visitors. That has changed since Arthur Kinmond Bell of Bell's Whisky made it into a woodland park with a visitor centre. The Gannochy Trust, which he founded in 1937, manages the park.

The original Scone Parish Church was built in 1624 at the Moot Hill, adjacent to the palace. An aisle of this old church was left standing when a new church was erected on another site in the palace grounds in 1784. When the old village of Scone was moved to its new site, the church was taken down and re-erected stone by stone to create as near a match as possible to the demolished building. This was sited on the edge of the village, on rising ground facing the Annaty Burn. It was completed in 1805 and some years later a large, handsome house was erected alongside as a manse. It became a private dwelling in the 1980s when the church opted for a more modest manse.

ESTABLISHED CHURCH MANSE : SCONE :

The re-erected church was soon struggling to accommodate the growing number of worshippers and so a new aisle was added in 1834. Nine years later the congregation was greatly reduced as the established church throughout Scotland was split in the dispute known as the Disruption, which led to the Free Church being set up. The passions that provoked such division had cooled by 1929 and the churches were reunited. This original church became known as Scone Old Parish Church to differentiate it from the others in the village. The churchyard is also the location of a large and ornate memorial to the botanist David Douglas, who met a terrible death at the age of 34. While looking for plants on the Sandwich Islands he fell into a pit dug by local people to trap wild bulls, but a bull had already been caught and it killed the helpless botanist.

The Annaty Burn was not always the pleasant tumbling stream it appears to be in this picture; it was sometimes a roaring torrent and on those occasions the Burnside could be an uncomfortable place to live. In July 1916, swollen by a spell of incessant rain, it burst its banks below the bridge and poured down the road, causing the front of a house to collapse. The date and the level of the flood have been carved on the wall of the large house on the left of this picture. It was not the first, or indeed the last, time the burn damaged Burnside properties, but the bank at the vulnerable bend has since been shored up with concrete to give some protection from future floods. The communal washing poles in the foreground are still in use, providing a more pleasing link with the past.

The Earl of Mansfield offered generous feus to encourage villagers to move to the new location. They also had large plots to grow food, but despite these advantages the new village was, to begin with, not particularly prosperous. Prior to their move from Old Scone, the people divided their time between handloom weaving and, in a season that lasted from February to August, salmon netting on the Tay. The site of the new village was less convenient for the salmon, and within a few years the weaving – which was not well paid anyway – was rendered unprofitable by the growth of industrial processes in towns and cities. Many Scone folk had to travel to the big textile factories in Perth to find employment, while others filled the pot by indulging in a wee spot of poaching! This view of the southern end of the village, from the ground now used for the cemetery, shows houses facing the Perth Road with those of the Burnside behind. The Perth Road buildings were demolished in 1959 to make way for new housing for elderly people.

Scone was admirably quick in erecting a memorial to those from the parish who died during the First World War. Made of Kemnay granite, it was sited close to the bridge at the southern end of the village and unveiled on 26 June 1920 by the Countess of Mansfield. The poignant ceremony was followed by piper William Keir playing the suitably haunting 'Flowers o' the Forest'. The money raised for the memorial more than covered the costs and the surplus funds were put towards the endowment of a district nurse for the Scone Parish Nursing Association. The burden of maintaining the memorial was taken on by the Parish Council. Thirty years later, on 3 September 1950, another ceremony was held at the memorial when 90-year-old Mrs Jane Mitchell unveiled the names added after the Second World War. Sadly, more have been added since, most recently that of a soldier killed in Iraq in 2003 while serving with the Black Watch.

The occupants of Picstonhill house and farm, on the southern edge of Scone, have from time to time been important to the life of the village and indeed to the wider community. In 1843, when the Free Church broke away from the Church of Scotland, James Stewart, the Picstonhill farmer, allowed the congregation to worship in a barn until a church could be erected. Building work was delayed by supporters of the established church who denied the breakaway congregation access for drawing stone between the quarry and the site of their church, but again James Stewart came to the rescue by making a haulage road across his land. The farmer who followed James Stewart at Picstonhill was Robert Mackenzie, who became noted for his progressive methods of farm management. He also had three remarkable sons: Robert, a well-known churchman, James, a world-renowned heart specialist, and William, Lord Amulree, who became an authority on industrial law and a King's Counsel.

The annual market in the old village of Scone was an event of some significance. People came from miles around to buy and sell produce and livestock. Games and other activities were held in conjunction with the main event, but when the village moved up the hill the fun and frolics continued while the market itself ceased to function in all but name. By the mid-nineteenth century Scone Market was little more than a local holiday; people dressed in their finery and strolled up and down the main street where stalls and barrows had been set up to induce them to spend their money.

Earlier in the century Perth poet, John Sinclair, described the scene:

Here mony a curious sicht gangs on:
See how the loons are sportin'!
Wha never ventured never won,
Haste, lads, and try your fortune!
The wheel, weel happit, eident rins,
Syne's steady's ony pillar;
Hark, round the roly-poly pins
A's busy makin' siller
In heaps this day.

By 1909/10, when the pictures on these two pages are thought to have been taken, Scone Market had become little more than a children's funfair with stalls, barrows and roundabouts set up at the end of Cross Street. The location will also have encouraged the continuance of another aspect of the old fair, the conspicuous consumption of strong drink, because the stalls have been set up right outside the Scone Arms, while just up Cross Street was the Cross Tavern, run at the time by an Ellen Henderson. The Scone Arms was not always known by that name, having formerly been the Green Tree Inn and Carmichael Arms.

When the village moved, the old stone cross remained *in situ*. The people protested and so, as a substitute, the Earl of Mansfield allowed them to take a tree trunk from his woods every year and erect it in the village. The forester usually wanted the villagers to have a poor specimen, but they never took the one he had in mind. The men arrived in the woods in numbers and by pretending to cut down any number of trees so distracted the man he didn't know which one they were taking. The prize was carried off in triumph, stripped of its bark, greased and set up with a cartwheel at the top; prizes were offered to anyone who could climb to the top. Rivalry between local lads and those from Perth who came to try their luck led to friction and fighting. The Countess of Mansfield sought to end this antisocial behaviour by having a replica stone cross made which was given to the village and erected at the junction of Cross Street and Abbey Road.

Abbey Road is seen here looking north from the cross in the mid-1920s before it was surfaced and the footpaths properly defined. Although known locally as the 'back road', it is more like a second main street running straight and true while the real main road takes a meandering course through the village. Further up on the left is the Robert Douglas Memorial Home, a complex of cottages and rest home for elderly people that was completed and occupied by 1933. It was one of many facilities to benefit from $1m bequeathed to the inhabitants of Scone for their health, welfare and well-being. It was left to the village in 1929 by Robert Douglas, the eldest son of John Douglas, founder of the village's jam factory (see page 43). He gained his early business experience in Scotland before leaving for America in 1887, at the age of 28. He settled in Rochester, New York and set up a fruit processing and packing company which developed into one of the largest concerns of its kind in the world. As a result of his bequest Scone became known as the 'lucky village' and the envy of Perthshire.

Further up Abbey Road is the church, latterly known as the West Church, which owed its origins to a ceremony at Gairney Bridge, near Kinross, in 1733, when the first Secession Church broke away from the established Church of Scotland. That church in turn split into factions and one of these formed a congregation in Old Scone in 1748. Its church building, like that of the Church of Scotland, was taken down and re-erected in the new village in 1810. The various factions of the Secession Church came together again as the United Presbyterian Church in 1847 and the Scone congregation erected a new church in 1885. After the union of the United Presbyterian and Free Churches in 1900 it was called the West Church and it kept that name after reunification with the Church of Scotland in 1929. When the congregation amalgamated with that of the Abbey Church in 1952 it became the church hall, but was turned into housing when a new hall was erected in Balformo Road.

Charles Hutchison JP of Crossview gifted fifteen acres of ground to the parish for use as a park. A corner of it was opened in August 1924 as a putting green, but the ceremony, presided over by Alexander Macduff of Bonhard, had to be held in the village hall because of bad weather. The green proved to be a popular facility, but when the Robert Douglas bequest gave the village the opportunity to expand the park's facilities in 1931 it had to vie for people's attention with many other attractions. Unable to stand the test of time, it fell into disuse. A suggestion in the early 1990s that it should be turned into a car park was greeted with outrage and instead, with the assistance of a grant from Perth and Kinross District Council, it was laid out as a memorial garden for David Douglas. Many of the species he discovered were incorporated into the planting scheme.

This little newsagents and stationery shop in Perth Road, diagonally opposite the Scone Arms, was run by a David Hutchison, although it is not known which, if either, of these two men he is. The picture, taken by Scone photographer William Stewart, almost certainly pre-dates 1900/1901, when the shop appears to have been taken over by a Christine Harris. Remarkably, given the decrepit appearance of the building, it seems to have survived and to have been extended, and is now used by an insurance broker.

Den, the Scots equivalent of the English word 'dene', means a narrow wooded valley, which at Scone is formed by the Annaty Burn and its tributaries. It has long been a place where the folk of the village have gone for a peaceful walk and so the Earl of Mansfield was acknowledging common popular usage when he conveyed by feu disposition the lower part of the Den to the County Council in 1952. The area also lay close to the new houses at Goshenbank and was intended to be used to provide recreational facilities for people from that area. The picture on the left is of the entrance to the Den, with the backs of buildings in Perth Road, while the other view shows the burn in more open country above the village.

Lignwood is a large Victorian mansion occupying a six-acre site on the corner of Perth and Bonhard Roads. It originally had three public rooms, four bedrooms, two with dressing rooms, cloakroom, bathroom, conservatory, two maids' rooms, maids' bathroom and two attic rooms. There was also a four-roomed entrance lodge, with an outside toilet. The first post office in the village apparently pre-dated the lodge on the site. At the time this picture was taken, the big house was inhabited by a Mr Edward Campbell, a man whose interest in local affairs included serving on the village hall committee. The Literary Association appears to have been the driving force behind the village hall, which was built in 1880 on a site in Queens Road gifted by Mr Murray-Graham of Murrayshall. Money was raised in a number of ways, including a bazaar held at Bonhard House, the home of Alexander Macduff. He was chairman of trustees from 1880 until 1920 when the hall was transferred to the Parish Council. Since then it has remained in local authority control while also receiving money from the Robert Douglas Foundation for renovation.

Inverannaty is a large house off Bonhard Road looking almost due west from an elevated site between the road and the Den. The location makes the name, which means 'at the mouth of the Annaty', somewhat inaccurate, but house names often defy explanation. Inverannaty appears to have been built about 1902 or 1903 and lived in for a few years by a John A. Robertson before becoming the home of Colonel George Ross Cavaye about 1907.

Halfway through the First World War Colonel Cavaye's occupancy of the house ended and at about the same time it appears to have become a convalescent home for wounded servicemen. It continued in that capacity for some years afterwards – at least until 1924, when this picture was taken. The two pictures offer a fascinating comparison of the garden when the house was new, and what it had grown into twenty years later when the trees had matured. The garden ground has since been reduced in size and some more modest houses built on it, but Inverannaty has survived and reverted to being a private dwelling.

The main road has always been busy. In the days of horse-drawn transport it was used by numerous carts and coaches transporting produce and people. Horses on long journeys could be watered at the Annaty Burn or changed for fresh animals at stabling in Cross Street. Scone was of course never served by a railway, so it remained reliant on road-based transport systems and when motor vehicles were developed the village was in an ideal location for garages. Drummond's at Murrayshall Road appears to have been established in the early 1920s and Keir's, in Perth Road, a few years later. Cameron Motors was set up in Perth Road in 1958 with a 10,000 sq ft car showroom. Its space for displaying up to 90 vehicles was claimed to be the largest in Scotland, but by the mid-1980s it had been turned into a furniture showroom – the largest complete house furnisher in Perthshire, according to T. & L. Smith who set it up! Other changes followed, but Keir's former garage is the only one still in the trade. Now shorn of petrol pumps, it is operated as the Scone Motor Company and Scottish Quad Bike Centre.

These pictures looking north along Perth Road date from the early twentieth century, when the trams were horse-hauled. In the main picture the horses appear to have deposited some pollution on the road, which sometimes caused just as much concern for people in those days as motor vehicle exhausts do today! The road surface is of beaten earth and stones, and appears to lack proper ditches, gutters or drains. It shows just why trams became popular, running on smooth rails which didn't require the entire road surface to be paved, only a bed of cobbles laid down the centre of the carriageway. Scone people campaigned long and hard to have improvements made to their roads and footpaths, and from these pictures it is easy to see why. The ill-defined beaten earth footpaths, particularly the one on the right, are in an even worse state than the road and will have alternated between mud and dust depending on the weather. The picture on the right was used as a postcard in 1907: the message reads 'We have had two great snowstorms this year … the country roads were impassable for bakers' vans etc.'

The tram rails were lifted in 1929, and the road (presumably along with the footpaths) was properly defined and surfaced in 'Trinidad asphalt', which, according to at least one critic, made the surface look 'more like a race track than a public road' (there's no pleasing some folk!). It is seen here in 1933 with a Dundee-registered car sitting outside a house next to the post office, which was built early in the twentieth century. As with all village post offices, it provided a vital service for local people, but in 1951 one man decided to help himself to the takings. He hid in the house until after closing time, but the sub-postmaster, Robert Beedie, heard a noise and went to investigate, and his 80-year-old father-in-law, Alexander Dewar, followed. They intercepted the intruder, who was leaving with a fistful of money. He hit both men with a wrench, but they grappled him to the floor and while they struggled Mr Beedie's daughter stepped over them to get to the phone, but before the police could arrive the man made his escape. He was arrested in Glasgow the following day. On a happier note, the post office was voted the best in Tayside in 1995.

The Scone and Perth Omnibus Company began operating horse-drawn buses between Scone and Perth in the 1860s, although it took a while for people to catch on to the opportunities the service had opened up. When they did, folk from Scone started to use it to go to work in Perth and folk from Perth began to move out of the crowded town to live in the country village. As passenger numbers increased, the idea of converting the service into one operated by trams began to grow, and in 1894 the Perth & District Tramway Company took over the bus company. They started running horse-drawn trams the following year. The new service, which took 25 minutes to go from Scone to Perth Cross, was inaugurated with a ceremonial run to and from Glasgow Road in Perth. The invited guests adjourned to the village hall for cake and wine on their return to Scone.

Initially the trams ran through the city centre to Rose Crescent on the Glasgow Road, which provided a direct link to Perth General Station, but in December 1898 the service was extended to Cherrybank. Perth Town Council watched the tramway's growing success with interest and in 1901 made the company an offer. It was refused, but they were tempted by a revised offer and two years later the tramway was sold to the council. They set about electrifying the system and the last horse-drawn tram ran on 31 October 1905. Three of the old cars were put to a new use as shelters and one of these, seen here, was at Scone. The main route for the electric cars was still between Scone and Cherrybank, running every fifteen minutes except for peak periods in the morning and evening, when it was every ten minutes.

It initially cost twopence to travel between Perth Cross and Scone, with the return fare only a halfpenny more. In 1918 fares were increased to stave off rising costs, but soon the trams were having to compete with a new rival. Motor bus services spread rapidly throughout the Perth area in the 1920s and late in the decade were operating in direct competition with the trams. It was a race the old worn out trams were always going to lose and they ceased to operate in 1929. They left a legacy in Scone. The original horse-drawn bus operators established their office, stables and depot in the village and this was taken over by the tramway company and then by Perth Town Council. During these different phases of ownership the depot was modified to take in the trams and enlarged when the system was electrified, with the trams running into the area formerly used as stabling. It remained as a bus depot for a time after the demise of the trams.

Scone. Free Church.

The Disruption, the schism that split the established Church of Scotland, was the result of a fundamental argument over who had the right to appoint a minister, a powerful patron or the congregation. It struck at the heart of Presbyterianism. In Scone the people who left the established church to join the new Free Church of Scotland built their first church in 1844. They also erected a school beside it, which was transferred to the School Board following the Education Act of 1872. The first church was demolished in 1886 and replaced the following year by a splendid new building made of red Dumfriesshire sandstone. Sometimes known as the 'red church', it was officially renamed the Abbey Church following the unification of the Free and United Presbyterian Churches in 1900. It retained this name when the United Free Church and the Church of Scotland reunited in 1929, but became known Scone New Church when the congregations of the West and Abbey Churches amalgamated in 1952.

Scone New Church faces Perth Road, on the corner with Balformo Road, which is seen here from the church tower in a view from the early 1930s. Two of the most dedicated supporters of the church, Mr W. Goodsman and his daughter Margaret, lived at Balformo House, across Balformo Road from the church. Margaret succeeded her father in his role as the congregation's treasurer and gifted the new church building to the congregation when it was completed in 1887. Scone Bowling Club is at the top of Balformo Road, where it turns into Union Road. Beyond that, in the distance, is Scone Woods on the left and the Stormont Road area on the right, which has since been developed with housing.

The foreground tree in this view of Angus Road looking towards the village beautifully frames the church tower and also marks the present-day entrance to the large pub/restaurant known as the Wheel Inn. It was originally Balformo House, where the Free Church's benefactors, the Goodsmans, lived. In 1964 it was turned into what its owners described as 'Scone's first-ever hotel' – a claim the proprietors of the early village inns might have disputed, had they still been around. It had six bedrooms, a dining room for 40 people, and gardens with views of the Sidlaw Hills. Guests could enjoy these while sitting on benches fashioned from an old cherry tree cut down during reconstruction. Those gardens are now much reduced by car parking and the old house has been almost completely engulfed by a space dedicated to the consumption of food and drink – what would the douce Free Church folk have thought of it?

The 61 ft high church tower gave photographers a splendid vantage point for pictures of the village. This one shows Angus Road as little better than a track heading north past the large house on the right, known as Ardmhor House. The gaps between these scattered houses have been filled with subsequent development which has since spread round the corner and out of the picture to the right. On the left, in Stormont Road, is the health centre, a facility which Scone's early residents might be surprised to see. A selling point for the new village was that it was on high ground, and that this was seen as being so much healthier than the old low-lying village on a fog-shrouded site close to the river. The environmental advantages of fresh clean air, new houses and uncluttered streets are well understood today, but if the old place was so unhealthy why did anyone stay there?

SCONE THISTLE F.C.

The old village of Scone used to hold a ball game on Shrove Tuesday from two o'clock until sunset. The contest was between married and unmarried men, and all, commons and gentry, were obliged to take part, or pay a fine. The first side to score three times was the winner. The ball could be handled but not kicked, and the saying that 'all was fair at the ball of Scone' suggests that some heavy tactics were employed. Scone Thistle play a different game. The team was formed in 1882, when football began as an organised sport in the Perth area, and although it has not been in continuous existence it is one of the few survivors from the early days and has achieved success in a variety of league and cup competitions over the years.

This team from the mid-1930s is: Back Row: R. Kennedy, J. Adamson, N. McPherson, R. Smith, J. Christie (Captain), J. MacGregor.
Front Row: C. Lannin, J. McWalters, C. Delbridge, J. Laing, J. Wallace.

The Robert Douglas bequest gave Scone the opportunity to increase the sporting and recreational facilities available in the public park. These included a children's playpark with swings, roundabout, seesaw, slide and paddling pool, and for adults there was a football park, a new pavilion, cricket ground, bowling green, a large boating pond and three tennis courts. Mrs Robert Douglas opened the new facilities on a wet day in July 1931. Tennis became one of the most popular sports as Scone people took to the courts with enthusiasm. Various trophies were donated – Sir Stanley Norie-Millar, for example, put up a cup for mixed doubles – and competition for these prizes was keen. Scone's tennis players also took part in the Perth and District League and some of the early players reached a high standard, with Duncan Campbell and Archibald Harris winning the men's doubles at the Scottish Public Courts Championships in 1936 and Andrew Harris coming runner-up in the singles.

Another village institution to benefit from the Douglas bequest was the Robert Douglas Memorial School, which was opened in August 1935 by Sir William Mackenzie, secretary of the Scottish Education Department. It replaced the Public School of 1876, which later became the Robert Douglas Institute. The front wall of the new school is adorned by a plaque made by Polish soldiers billeted in the village during the Second World War. The troubles of war were receding by the time this Primary 4 class attended the school in 1963. Fading memories also mean that, regrettably, some names are missing from this list and others may not be wholly correct:

Back Row: Henry Conn, Adam Easton, Ian Blackley, David Rossiter, Stewart Donaldson, Graham Dow, Kenneth Gabreck, Alastair Clifford, Jim Dewar, Derek Mitchell, Jeremy Duncan, Ian Wilkie.

Middle Row: Ralph Tilston, Cherry Guild, ?, Susan Haddow, Alison McLauchlan, Fiona Parker, ?, Daphne Forbes, Corinne McMahon, Michael Taylor.

Front Row: Penelope Bell, Linda Davidson, Muriel Thain, Evelyn Farquharson, Rhona Dickie, Gillian Forman, Alison Cation, Jane Cumming, Alison Urquhart, Edna May Robertson.

This view of the village taken from the vicinity of Bonhard Road shows the houses of Myrtle Place on the right and the jam factory (or 'jeely works') in the centre, although when this picture was taken in the late 1940s it was not making jam. The factory was started in the 1880s by John Douglas who, while selling produce door-to-door from his van, began to realise that there was a market for jams and jellies. The business went from strength to strength and the bill on the right, dated 1900, gives some insight into its activities. It details the sale of gooseberry jelly, marmalade and strawberry jam, and although this was a serious business, somebody must have had a sense of humour to select the telegraphic address 'Jam, Scone', shown in the top left-hand corner. It was clever too, because customers would certainly remember it. The works was bought in 1927 by J. S. Smith, who also made confectionery at the factory, but production had ceased before the Second World War, when the buildings were used for storage and a billet for Black Watch soldiers. They were bought in 1946 by W. N. Lindsay of Leith and later the same year by the Angus Milling Company, who used them for drying grain, the manufacture of animal feeds and agricultural merchandising.

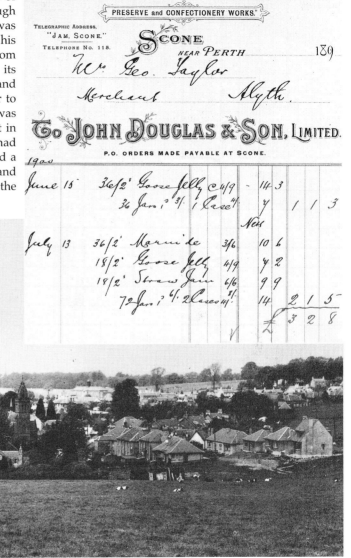

The Angus Milling Company that took over the jam factory produced Peter Pan oats – a marketing man's nightmare. How do you sell a product intended to make children grow up healthy and strong when it is named after the boy who never grew up? They were based at the Meikle Mill in Kirriemuir, which was formerly operated by a landowner under a system known as thirlage. It is probable that this mill at Bonhard was operated under the same system. Such mills were a big investment and to ensure their use the landowner tied or thirled the tenancies of farmers to the mill so that they were obliged to have their grain ground there. They also had to help with repairs and pay the miller and landowner with part of their meal. Farmers resented these impositions, and the eventual reduction in oats as the principal foodstuff saw the demise of many mills, although often farmers had to buy out their thirlage to be free of it.

The Jacobean style of architecture gives Bonhard House an air of antiquity, but it is of no great age, having been built about 1849 on the site of an earlier, ruined house, or castle, known as Springfield. A ruined doocot nearby was probably associated with the old structure, because the skewputs – the terminal stones of the crow-stepped gables – were carved with the date 1709. The lands of Bonhard were acquired by a Macduff, a descendant of a Strathbraan family whose estates had been confiscated and the head of the house hanged for associations with the Ruthvens at the time of the Gowrie Conspiracy in 1600. Macduff carefully rebuilt the family fortunes, eventually acquiring the lease of Perth Mills and, with the money from running them, was able to buy Bonhard and build the house. The Macduffs' hold on Bonhard was weakened when the heir, Captain Alexander Macduff, was killed during the First World War. His father, also Alexander, sold a number of the farms and, when he died in the 1930s, whisky merchant Matthew Gloag acquired Bonhard. A splendid garden centre now operates in the grounds.

Murrayshall, a large mansion about a mile to the east of the main village, was the property of Major Andrew J. G. Murray-Graham when it was the scene of a terrible fire tragedy in 1925. A spark from a drawing room fireplace is thought to have set the carpet alight. The blaze was discovered at four o'clock in the morning when it was already out of control. Two maids asleep in the nursery above the drawing room and the four-year-old heir to the estate perished, despite valiant efforts by a footman to rescue them. The telephone was not working properly so the fire engine had to be summoned by the chauffeur driving fast into Perth and even when the brigade arrived they could not get sufficient water pressure until a second unit arrived. The house was destroyed, but was rebuilt after Sir Francis Norie-Millar, managing director of General Accident Assurance, bought the estate in 1927. In 1974 it was bought by two Scone businessmen who planned to turn the house into a leisure centre, with a golf course in the grounds. It has since become a hotel with two golf courses.

Murrayshall Estate ran to 460 acres and included three arable farms, parks, gardens and woodland plantations. Neighbouring Balcraig, by comparison, was small at only 130 acres, of which 80 were arable and the remainder was flower and vegetable gardens and hill pasture. The mansion, which is thought to date from about 1842, was erected by the Misses Mercer and aligned to give views to the west, to Gorthy on the distant Braes of Fowlis. John Dewar of Dewar's Whisky was a tenant at Balcraig before he became Lord Provost of Perth. The house comprised four reception rooms, eight family bedrooms, one dressing room, five servants' rooms, three bathrooms and servants' hall. There were also houses for the chauffeur and gardener, two garages, stable, bothy and byres. It was opened as a hotel in 1982 which aimed to provide guests with fine cuisine and outdoor activities such as croquet and bowls on the lawn, tennis and pony-trekking. The venture proved unsuccessful and Balcraig reverted to being a private house.

Although the Air Navigation Act in 1920 started a debate, the idea of establishing an airport for Perth received little support until the government announced an expansion of the RAF in the 1930s. A relatively fog-free site was selected at Newlands and 250 acres of ground was purchased. Work to prepare the airfield began in June 1935 and the first aircraft took off in January the following year. More ground was acquired before its formal opening as Perth's municipal aerodrome in June 1936. Initially the landing strip had a grass surface, but regular flights were started to Renfrew (for Glasgow), Inverness via Aberdeen, and London via Newcastle, Leeds and Doncaster. The RAF also started training pilots and this function became the airfield's primary function during the Second World War. After the war Perth Town Council sold the airfield to Airwork Ltd, who continued to develop it as a training facility, a function it has performed ever since.